Haunted Places

Exploring The Creepiest Places On Earth: Don't Even Think About It...

Volume 2

Table of Contents

Introduction 4

Chapter 1 The Haunting of Old Faithful Inn 9

Chapter 2 The Prison Spirits 13

Chapter 3 The Children of Ancient Ram Inn 17

Chapter 4 Haunted Guests of Banff Springs 21

Chapter 5 The Unwell of Changi Hospital 25

Chapter 6 The Demon of Sallie House 28

Chapter 7 Eternal Wanderers 32

Chapter 8 The Insane Sanatorium 36

Chapter 9 The Haunting of the Dolls 40

Chapter 10 The Whispers of London's Tower 44

Chapter 11 The Haunted Secrets of Skirrid Inn 48

Chapter 12 The Demon of the Close 52

Conclusion 55

My Other Books 56

Would you like some free books?

Yes that's right, we send free books out to our subscribers every single week!

If you think that sounds pretty awesome, then visit our website at the end of this book and sign up!

All you have to do then, is keep an eye on your inbox for the next free books for the week.

Enjoy!

Introduction

Creepy places are everywhere. They often don't look too creepy on the outside, but once you dive into the history, listen to some of the reports of what people have seen or heard, or experience some of the events for yourself, you begin to realize just how many creepy places there are on this planet...

Some places are known to be haunted. There are countless stories that have been passed down through the years combined with the modern reports that are added to these tales at an alarming rate. There are places advertised in movies and on TV with famous ghost hunters and paranormal seekers, and there are word of mouth legends passed from locals to visitors.

Then there are places that are lesser known. People have heard of the sites, they know that they are old, but they have no idea of the tragedies or tales that have taken place there. Walls that hold secrets no one could bear to see, lakes that bury lives everyone has forgotten about.

Castles that tell tales far more intense than anything you could see or read in dramas. Yes, the world itself is so rich in secrets, we can only begin to scratch the surface as we dive into some of these stories full of facts that are stranger than fiction...

Paranormal events are rife in these places, whether they be residual hauntings from prisoners convicted of treason, or victims of murders and terrible crimes who continue to walk and haunt the halls of towers, castles, and inns.

In this book, we are going to look at a dozen of the best hauntings which take place around the world today, from England and Scotland to Singapore and Mexico and eerie sights in between, this book is full of true tales of hauntings, sightings, and paranormal activity like you have never heard before.

Are you ready to dive into the unknown, and explore a haunted world you had no idea existed? Then read on and discover things so out of this world you couldn't imagine them even in your darkest of dreams...

© **Copyright 2016 by Roger P. Mills - All rights reserved.**

This document is geared towards providing exact and reliable information in regards to the topic and issue covered. The publication is sold with the idea that the publisher is not required to render accounting, officially permitted, or otherwise, qualified services. If advice is necessary, legal or professional, a practiced individual in the profession should be ordered.

- From a Declaration of Principles which was accepted and approved equally by a Committee of the American Bar Association and a Committee of Publishers and Associations.

In no way is it legal to reproduce, duplicate, or transmit any part of this document in either electronic means or in printed format. Recording of this publication is strictly prohibited and any storage of this document is not allowed unless with written permission from the publisher. All rights reserved.

The information provided herein is stated to be truthful and consistent, in that any liability, in terms of inattention or otherwise, by any usage or abuse of any policies, processes, or directions contained within is the solitary and utter responsibility of the recipient reader. Under no circumstances will any legal responsibility or blame be held against the publisher for any reparation, damages, or monetary loss due to the information herein, either directly or indirectly.

Respective authors own all copyrights not held by the publisher.

The information herein is offered for informational purposes solely, and is universal as so. The presentation of the information is without contract or any type of guarantee assurance.

The trademarks that are used are without any consent, and the publication of the trademark is without permission or backing by the trademark owner. All trademarks and brands within this book are for clarifying purposes only and are the owned by the owners themselves, not affiliated with this document.

Roger P. Mills

Roger is a non-fiction author that enjoys writing about our worlds conspiracy theories, true paranormal stories and ghost stories. Over the years it has always staggered him as to how many unexplained mysteries there are in history.

A small town in Romania is where Roger likes to call home with his wife and dog. Here he finds the inspiration to write and explore all the unusual happenings of our world.

If you're into unexplained phenomena, the paranormal and conspiracies that have happened in the past and continue to happen, then be sure to check out his books.

Check out his other books here.

https://www.amazon.com/Roger-P.-Mills/e/B01LE0GL52/ref=sr_ntt_srch_lnk_2?qid=1482114954&sr=1-2

Chapter 1
The Haunting of Old Faithful Inn

Inns and lodges are some of the most haunted buildings on the planet. Perhaps this is because of all the people who have passed through, perhaps it's because spirits enjoy watching people who are still living their lives…

Regardless of the reason, it seems the inns and lodges around the planet carry the most paranormal stories.

One such story is found in the Old Faithful Inn in Yellowstone Park. This Inn stands near the famous Old Faithful Geyser, and has seen its fair share of events through the years. Along with these events have come hauntings and paranormal activity, which many modern day visitors have witnessed.

The most common, and perhaps the creepiest sighting is of the headless bride, who is doomed to walk the crow's nest high above the balconies, carrying her head under her arm. This ghostly apparition is the spirit of a teenage girl who ran away to marry against her parent's wishes.

The year was 1915 in New York City, and she was the daughter of a wealthy man who had betrothed her to another gentleman who was a family friend. But, the girl was rebellious, and she wanted to marry one of the servants in the household… a man who was much older than herself.

Her father, concerned that the servant was only after the family's money, didn't approve of the wedding, but his daughter didn't care. She told her father she was going to marry the servant whether he wanted her to or not, and there was nothing he could do to stop her.

The situation was quickly becoming a scandal, and the man could see that there was little he could do about the situation. He loved his daughter, but he had to make a decision...

Not wanting to lose his daughter over the marriage, her father offered to pay them both a large sum of money on their wedding day, with the condition that they would leave New York and never return.

The daughter, happy that she had won the battle, agreed to the terms, and their wedding day came.

The newlyweds decided to spend their honeymoon at the Old Faithful Inn in Yellowstone Park, as that was one of the nicest places of the time. But, her father's fears soon proved to be valid, and her new husband spent much of their money before they had even reached Montana.

Refusing to believe she had made a mistake, the two of them continued on to the lodge, where they chose one of the biggest suites in the entire Inn. Yet his spending continued, and before long they were out of money...

Then the fights started, and the guests would listen to many a heated argument between the two. Things would hit the walls, there would be loud banging noises, and glass would be shattered, but the couple continued to uphold their relationship in front of the other guests at the lodge.

But they needed money, and it wasn't long before the girl called her father and asked if he could send them more funds. Her father, knowing that this was going to happen, refused to send them any more money, reminding his daughter of their bargain.

Days went by, and the fighting continued.

Until one day, right after a bad fight, the husband came out of the room, walked down the steps, and right out the front door.

He never returned.

The guests and staff felt that the girl may have needed some time to herself after the incident, realizing what must have happened between them. But, days went by, and she never came out. In fact, there were no sounds at all coming from within the room, so the staff decided it might be a good idea for them to go in and check on her.

But nothing could prepare them for what they found...

The girl was in the bathtub, dressed in her wedding gown, decapitated... The tub was full of blood and water... but they couldn't find her head. Not wanting to make a scene, the staff cleaned up the mess, but again, her head wasn't ever found.

A few weeks later, a man was doing routine maintenance in the attic and could smell something terrible. Tearing up the floorboards, they discovered the girl's head. The staff members were horrified at what they discovered, and everyone hoped the incident would pass over quickly. Life went on as usual, until the year 1975.

A night watchman was walking through the ground story of the Inn, enjoying a quiet shift. Suddenly, he thought he saw something up in the crow's nest, so he took a step forward. He immediately realized what it was, and felt terrified...

It was a woman standing in the crow's nest, though there was no way she could have gotten up there. She was dressed in a white wedding dress, but the dress was soaked in blood. And to make matters worse, she was headless...

Instead of on her shoulders where it ought to have been, she was carrying her head beneath one of her arms. She stood silently in the nest, causing the watchman to flee in terror. He had heard the tale of the murder, as everyone who came to work for the lodge did, but he had never believed in the existence of ghosts, and was terrified at the sight of the woman in the rafters.

At first, some called him crazy, others said that he had made the story up for attention, and some claimed he was only trying to scare the visitors or have a story to tell them when they asked if the place was haunted.

But, he wasn't the only one to report seeing this ghostly apparition. She has appeared on the stairwell leading up to the second floor, she has appeared walking down the halls of the Inn, and she has since appeared in the crow's nest on multiple occasions.

Yet every time she appears, there's one thing that's always the same, and that's the fact she always has her head under her arm.

She never tries to engage any of the visitors, she never moves things around within the lodge or any of the rooms, she just walks silently by, forever drifting through the ancient beams and rafters that hold the grand building...

Chapter 2
The Prison Spirits

In addition to inns and lodges, it seems prisons are another frequently haunted structure. There are many terrible things that went on in old prisons, and some of the poor souls who were a part of them remain trapped within the walls to this day.

Some of these people were guilty of heinous crimes, others had made mistakes and ended up in the same place as all the rest. But, fate isn't selective, and there are a number of spirits from these prisoners still wandering the halls to this very day.

Built in 1829, the Eastern Penitentiary held 253 cells. Regardless of the crime the prisoner committed, there was only one person per cell. The goal of this prison was to place each person in solitary confinement for the entirety of their sentence... in the hopes that this would cause them to reflect upon themselves and what they did, and find forgiveness.

But, even in the early stages of the prison, there were rumors that the place was haunted. Some claimed that it was purely the effects of solitary confinement on the human mind, but there are a number of others who feel there is more to it than that...

But this plan backfired as solitary confinement led a number of prisoners to go insane. Even Al Capone was held within the walls for eight months of his life, and had to endure the same level of solitary confinement as the rest of the prisoners. Though he was sane when he went into the cell, he began to call out to the guards, convinced that one of his victims was coming into the cell to haunt him.

Though some believe that this is one of the earliest known hauntings about the prison, many others claim it was a result of being placed in solitary confinement for so long, so the prison re-thought its methods. Other reports of sightings began to crop up with the prisoners, and each one sounded different from the rest.

Concerned, the prison decided to change how it handled the men, but it wasn't long before more problems began to arise...

Soon, they were allowing two or three prisoners in a cell at a time, giving them all plenty of opportunity for human interaction. But, this didn't solve all their problems, as the warden of the prison was a cruel man, and often did things to the prisoners that was far beyond their crimes.

It has been recorded that he would starve men for days at a time, or have them tightly tied to chairs that resembled barber's chairs. He would have them secured in place so they couldn't move any part of their body, then leave them to stay in the same place for days, resulting in numerous deaths.

Other prisoners he would have thrown into icy water in the winter months, then tie them to the walls of the prison to freeze.

It seemed there would be no end to these torturous treatments, and it is widely believed that it is the pain and suffering that took place within the walls which led to it being haunted.

Yet there was a glimmer of hope, and the prison was officially closed in 1971.

Once closed, it appeared as though the prison became frozen in time. Items were still left lying about the building, there was still litter and garbage from the days of operation within the cells. There were still beds and other furnishings in the cells, and the whole place looked as though it had been left in a hurry, and without much care.

As you can imagine, this brought paranormal seekers and ghost hunters in from all over the country, each one searching for any proof that the place was really haunted.

The prison had housed more than seventy thousand prisoners during the time of operation, and many of them were exposed to the brutality of the harsh warden. Though the prison re-opened as a museum, there are still many paranormal events taking place within the walls.

In 2007, two sisters walked through the prison together, exploring the history it had to offer and trying to get a glimpse into the past and what went on there.

But strange things started happening. Footsteps were heard running through the halls, but as they rounded the corner, there would be no one there. There were whispers in several of the rooms when it was just the two of them present, and in some of the cells, they could even hear some people crying out in pain or agony...

Beginning to feel uneasy, the two sisters decided they had had enough, and were getting ready to leave, when they began to see things on the walls. Shadows of people strapped to chairs, shadows of people strapped to the walls.

There were shadows of a person watching them, but when they walked past the room, there was no one there.

They decided it was best for them to leave the prison, but even as they walked through the halls and back to the main lobby, neither one of them could shake the feeling they were being watched and followed...

They would keep a sharp eye out for anyone or anything that could be fooling them, but it was clear they were the only ones in many of the areas, and that there was no way they were mistaking what they were seeing, for something it wasn't.

And these two aren't the only ones to have had such experiences.

Many report shadows moving on the walls without explanation, there are shouts and whispers, and again those cries of agony.

Though not everyone who walks through the prison has had these experiences, there have been enough reported sightings that it's clear there are prisoners within the walls who will never leave, forever doomed to sit and watch the world taking place around them, but never being able to take part in it themselves...

Chapter 3
The Children of Ancient Ram Inn

There's just something enchanting about England no matter what you think about it. It's rolling green hills, elegant structures, beautiful scenery... it's enough to make you forget about all your problems and lose yourself for a moment without even trying.

But for all the richness of the land and with all the history that surrounds the countryside, it's of little surprise to learn that England is one of the most paranormal places on the planet. From haunted woods and lakes to houses with secrets like you could never imagine, England is the place to go if you would like to experience something paranormal for yourself.

In this chapter, we are going to stop by the Ancient Ram Inn located in Gloucestershire, England. The building is so haunted, it is said that many of the locals will refuse to walk by it at night, opting for out of the way paths around the back or a few streets over.

But what happened here that caused such a haunting? What are the events that cause people to believe that it's haunted?

Let's dive deeper and I'll show you...

The building was erected in the year 1145 by a group of men who also built the church which stands on the other side of the street. It is believed that these men were staying in the inn during the time of the construction of the church, and that the pastor resided there after.

It didn't remain a priest's quarters for long, and was converted into an inn and tavern until the year 1968. Throughout the years, the Inn saw many temporary and permanent residents, though now it is only occupied by one permanent resident by the name of John Humphries, who purchased the building from a brewery.

Though many people have sought to have the Inn demolished over the years, Humphries is adamant that it stays in place.

Inside the Inn, there are a number of narrow corridors, stairwells, and room after room that chills you to the bone. The floorboards are old and worn, but there are places in which the original boards are still in place.

But it isn't just the look of the building that will strike a nerve, it's the feel of the building as well. There's a sense of foreboding in the structure that will strike a chill into anyone's heart, no matter how little they believe in the existence of ghosts. Though windows are open, letting in the cold countryside air, many who have been inside the building leave quickly, explaining that the air is awful, with a dark, heavy feeling...

But interestingly enough, they don't consider it to be awful in that it smells, but almost like there's a darkness to the air itself that reaches into your innermost parts, again, regardless of how you feel about the paranormal.

It's not just the air that's haunting, however, as many parts of the structure hold different kinds of hauntings, with many people reporting different things based on where they were in the Inn at the time.

As you walk into the door, the first room you enter is known as the Men's Kitchen. It is known to stand on a pagan burial place, and over the decades, there have been reports of cries and screams coming from the room, though no one is in there. The sound of a baby crying is the most frequently reported sound, and there haven't been children in the structure in years...

Many people have reported that not all the spirits in the structure are friendly, and some have been thrown up the stairs as they were ascending... even during the daylight hours.

A photograph taken on this staircase in the year 1999 revealed a white mist that somewhat resembled a human form standing on the stairs, and appeared to be facing the camera...

There are several stories to this Inn, but perhaps the most terrifying room in the entire house can be found on the third floor, in a room that is known as the Bishop's room.

Again, windows may be left open, and the air is allowed to move through the place freely, but there is a dark feeling in this room, and once you enter, you begin to feel uneasy, and a terrible sense that something bad is about to happen.

It's reported that a woman who was trying to close the door to the room was lifted from her feet and thrown violently across the room, though no one in the room could see anything around her when it happened.

Ghostly apparitions appear in various locations throughout the building, dressed in medieval attire and walking from one side of the room to the other. They appear anywhere in the house, and can walk right through the walls.

Whispers and voices run through the walls, and many people have reported hearing shouts echoing through the halls, but perhaps the most disturbing report of all is the screaming of a man in the main living area of the home. It is reported that this man was brutally murdered by having his head held inside the fireplace…

The grounds are rife with paranormal activity as the ghostly apparition of a shepherd and his dog appear late at night from time to time, and a beautiful young maiden often appears next to one of the rooms, trying to get inside the Inn through the window.

But the saddest room in the building is up in the attic, where a young girl, the reported daughter of the innkeeper in the 1500s, was brutally murdered by a man who hated her father. To this day, those who stay in the upper rooms of the Inn report hearing the screams of a young girl and the sound of something being dragged across the floor…

It can be a difficult decision to enter this inn to experience the paranormal for yourself, but if you ever have the opportunity, I highly suggest you take it. Stepping inside this Inn is like taking a step back in time, and getting to experience things that happened hundreds of years ago.

However, it's evident that these spirits are incredibly active, and considering some of the events that have transpired within the walls, it's safe to say that they aren't all friendly, so any visit to the Inn must be made with extreme caution.

Perhaps the Inn will be torn down one day, but until then, the spirits who wander the halls and go through the walls will continue on their infinite course, undeterred by people who may be watching…

Chapter 4
Haunted Guests of Banff Springs

When you think about Canada, you think of lakes and trees, maple syrup, and perhaps leaves. What few people think about are ghosts or paranormal events, but even Canada has its fair share of hauntings in the world, and now we will take a look at one of the biggest... and creepiest hauntings the country can boast.

Alberta, Canada has a lot to offer to the world, and it remains one of the top tourist hot spots in the entire country. The Banff Springs Hotel, which is nestled in Alberta, is also a tourist favorite, though there is far more happening in that building than what meets the eye...

The structure was erected in the year 1888 when the railroad was finally completed through the area. A man by the name of William Van Horne felt that it would be the perfect place for people to stay as they travelled through the area, and the immense building was put in place.

This first structure was built entirely out of wood, but there is mystery in its walls. No one knows why, but there was a room constructed within the hotel that had no windows and no known doors.

There doesn't appear to be any use for this room, and no one is sure why it was there in the first place. It doesn't appear on any of the plans, and it doesn't appear to serve any real purpose for anything with the hotel.

There are natural hot springs in the area, beautiful scenery as far as the eye can see, and all the wonders the Rocky

Mountains has to offer, making this an ideal location for anyone who was traveling through the area.

But the building was not without its difficulties, and in the year 1926, the entire structure burned to the ground when a fire of an unknown origin spread through its halls. Though the fire was a tragedy, it soon proved it was worse to not have the hotel in the area, and it wasn't long before there was talk of building another... stronger establishment.

As a result, another hotel was built in the exact location as the first, only it was built with stone walls as thick as walls used in a castle, giving the structure a lot more support than the original had.

The newer structure looks so medieval that many who have visited it have dubbed it to be "the Castle of the Rockies". And a castle it proves to be.

Though it was rebuilt after it had burned to the ground, there are still paranormal accounts tied to that one secret room. No one knows for sure why this is, but there is plenty of speculation.

Ghostly apparitions appear around this room in the form of young children, and voices can be heard in this area, too, though it's hard to understand what the voices are actually saying.

The majority of the hauntings within the hotel seem to be results of tragedies... though this hotel hasn't had many, the tragedies which did occur have resulted in hauntings throughout the building.

Though there is a lot of mystery in connection to the mystery room, there is another room that holds a lot more haunting, room 873. This room was the site of a terrible tragedy, and as a result, spirits linger...

It is said that this room once housed a family of 3... a mother, a father, and a little girl. But, during their stay in the hotel, they were all brutally murdered by a masked intruder. The police were notified, and the hotel staff did their best to clean the room... However, as strange as it was, there was no way they could get the fingerprints off the mirror. They scrubbed as much as they could, but the fingerprints would always appear 24 hours later...

Since then, there are reports of seeing all 3 members of this family throughout the hall, but especially in and around that room. There are times when they appear together, then there are times when they appear separately. There doesn't appear to be any real pattern to how they appear, but guests have reported seeing them all at various times.

Another tragedy which occurred in the hotel happened unexpectedly, and the resulting haunting is one that brings sadness to all who see her...

A wedding was to take place in the lobby of the hotel, and the two young lovers got ready in each of their own rooms. But, when the time came for them to walk the aisle, the bride came out of her room and sadly tripped on her dress as she was walking down the stairs.

She fell down the entire flight, breaking her neck at the bottom. She died almost instantly.

To this day, you can still see this bride walking up and down the stairs, dressed in her same wedding gown and looking onward with anticipation, only the spirit's face is marred with a sadness, as though she knows she is forever doomed to walk the steps and never truly be joined to her love.

The final residual haunting of the hotel is seen on the top floor, alone. There is a man who served in the hotel for many years, from the time he was old enough to work until he finally passed away in the upper rooms.

No one knows what caused his death, but he can still be seen walking around in the upper rooms, though there isn't any real pattern to where he is or when he's going to be there. Guests who have seen him, report not realizing that he isn't a spirit until they try to touch him.

He shuffles past, and they talk to him, but he keeps moving. If they are concerned that he didn't hear them and pursue him, or if they try to touch his arm or shoulder, he simply vanishes into thin air, without leaving any trace behind.

Of course, there are reports of other ghostly apparitions appearing in various locations around the hotel, and as the hotel has been standing for nearly one hundred years, there is little doubt that people have been seeing things for a very long time...

Chapter 5
The Unwell of Changi Hospital

Hospitals are one of the most haunted places on the planet, and it seems the abandoned ones are rife with paranormal activity. Then, when there are more events that take place around the hospital, there is even more opportunity for it to become haunted.

That is what happened with the Changi Hospital in Singapore. Singapore is filled with mystery as it is, but when you hear just how strange this hospital is, you will never view the area the same again.

The Changi hospital was originally constructed in the early part of the 1900s, and was a popular place. The medical staff knew what they were doing, the patients received the best treatment, and the healthcare was good.

Though it was primarily under the control of the British, the hospital saw a lot of rough times right from the beginning. Then, when WWII shook the planet, foreigners took control of the entire area.

But then things began to decline as war broke out across the world. In 1942, the Japanese had occupation of Singapore, and they took control of the hospital, but they didn't treat it as a hospital, but rather as a commune to torture prisoners of war.

Millions of men were placed under torture in these walls, as Japanese soldiers would use instruments they found within the hospital as instruments of torture. Men would be tied to the beds and surgical tools would be used on them, people would be tortured with needles, and men would be beaten...

It has been rumored that men's heads would be severed and impaled on stakes, then left out in front of the hospital as intimidation to people in the area. Anyone who was considered a threat to the soldiers during this time underwent this kind of treatment, and were all subjected to the same fate.

After the war, the hospital was returned to British control, but it was never thought of the same way again. No one wanted to open it back up as a hospital, and though many people tried to bring it back to the way it used to be, it was during this time that the paranormal reports started coming in...

Many of the patients and visitors reported hearing screaming coming through the halls, sounds of torture coming from empty rooms, and shadows running along the walls. The more this went on, the less people wanted to go to the hospital, and the fewer patients there were to treat.

During this time, the hospital changed ownership several times. Many people tried to refurbish it and turn it into something else, but no one was able to bring out the best in the building.

Eventually, the place was abandoned entirely.

In 2006, the building was put up for lease, and a company took control of it, wanting to turn it into a luxury resort. Though the plans seemed to be going well, they fell through at the last minute and nothing ever came of the idea.

The entire area of Changi began gaining popularity for its haunting, and several film crews were in the area trying to film horror and action documentaries.

Several of these people reported hearing ghostly voices coming from within the rooms of the hospital, while others reported hearing screams and shouting. Some people have reported seeing bloody soldier apparitions walking through the halls, while others report seeing a young boy who sits on the stair cases and watches the activity, but never says anything to anyone...

Some of the visitors have tried to engage the apparitions, others feel terrified when they see them. There are those who say they disappear when you draw near to them, then others who claim they have been touched by one of the spirits at one point.

Though the sightings are real, there are many more reports of the terrible and haunting sounds that fill the halls of the place.

There are sightings of ghosts walking around the grounds of the hospital, and several sightings of shadow people, even in the daylight hours. Some have even claimed to catch these people on camera, but it's hard to validate those stories.

Overall, the hauntings appear to be visual primarily, but there are instances when there has been physical contact between the spirits and the people in the hospital.

Several film crews who were in the hospital reported that their gear would mysteriously fall when no one was in the room, or that it would feel as though there was another presence in the room. There are reports of feeling like hands are on their backs or grabbing at their hair, and one man reported he was pushed from behind as he exited one room in the building.

Though to this day the hospital is primarily abandoned, it's an excellent location to visit if you want to see anything paranormal for yourself. Keep your eyes open and watch the walls, you never know what you're going to find...

Chapter 6
The Demon of Sallie House

There are some hauntings that fill buildings with rich history, there are hauntings that fill areas of tragedy, and there are hauntings that occur where many people have passed through.

But there are times when a haunting is in a much smaller area, and for a much smaller reason. Hauntings such as these often occur when a tragedy takes place in the location, and that the spirit is still lingering in the area.

Then there are times when there is no apparent reason for an apparition to be in a building at any given time. Sometimes, they seem to just appear out of nowhere and stay around for years. Though we may never know why or where these apparitions come from, why is not always the important thing.

Some spirits such as this are hostile, and can be referred to as demons rather than ghosts. In this next haunting, we are going to look at a spirit who is more demonic in nature than ghostly.

Sometimes the only thing that really matters is that they are there.

The Sallie house, located in Atchison, Kansas, is one of the most terrifying haunted houses in the entire United States, or perhaps even the world. There are some who claim that the hauntings that take place in this area are either demonic spirits who are seeking to harm those who come into the house, or spirits who are residual from people who have lived there, and are now seeking help.

This house was originally constructed in the early 1900s. The house is so named for a little girl by the name of Sallie, and this is the name the first owners of the house gave to the spirit of the little girl that haunted the place.

At first, they weren't sure if the child spirit was there to haunt them, or if she was there to warn them of the evil spirits contained within the walls.

The original family who moved into the house was comprised of a mother and father, and two little children, a boy and a girl. This family lived in the house for years, and eventually the descendants lived out their days in the house as well.

When the final owner died, the house was transferred from owner to owner and boarder to boarder. But, as strange as it was, no one ever stayed in the house very long, and there weren't ever many records of people who lived in the place. They all had their reasons for moving out so quickly, buy it never appeared there was any real reason when the house was examined later on.

There was only one tenant who was able to stand the house's strange activities, and she lived in the house for the longest period of time since the original family who owned it. Though this woman by the name of Ethel didn't seem to experience any of the strange events on her own person, there were many reports of others who stayed in the house being attacked in some way.

A man by the name of Tom who lived in the house for only three months sustained a broken leg after mysteriously falling down the steps. Visitors to the house also sustained various minor injuries, from cuts and scrapes to bruises, but no one realized what was happening until later...

And it has never seemed relevant whether the visitors were actually living in the house or if they were simply investigating the house for one reason or another. Even those who were in the house looking for paranormal activity sustained a variety of cuts and scrapes, though they didn't notice them happening at the time.

One investigator walked through the house searching for paranormal activities, and thought he had left unscathed, but upon waking the next day, he found that he had several large bruises on the back of his neck and a large burn mark on the bottom of his foot.

He hadn't noticed any of these things when he was in the house, nor had he noticed it when he was going throughout his evening. It was only when he woke the next day that he realized he had been injured, and had the proof on his body.

But the haunting hasn't been entirely invisible. There are plenty of reports of full body apparitions, sightings of strange people or animals, and strange animal sounds in the walls...

There are reports of scratching on the walls or in the hallway, and weird footsteps in the halls. Even when there is only one person living there at a time, there are strange sounds coming from all areas of the house.

The apparitions appear anywhere, and can appear at any time. Many of the sightings do take place at night, but the strange scratching in the halls and in the walls occurs at any time of the day, including when the house is filled with visitors.

There have been several reports of multiple people sustaining injuries at the same time, and there have been other reports of only one person in a group being injured when the rest of them were just fine. There doesn't seem to be any real selection that goes on among the group, and people of all ages and both genders have sustained these injuries.

The little girl who was named Sallie is still seen from time to time, but there is no consistency of when or where she will be.

Due to the violent nature of the apparitions in the house, it is strongly suspected that this house is possessed by demons rather than spirits of those who have lived there in the past. While there is very little known about the girl named Sallie, people still argue as to what her purpose has been in the entire sequence of events.

It may never be confirmed where this paranormal little girl came from or why she has chosen this house, but as long as this house stands, it's certain that there will be a lot more paranormal events taking place within the walls...

Chapter 7
Eternal Wanderers

As we have seen before, there is something simply haunting about London, England. The entire country is rich in history... and paranormal activity, and it doesn't seem to matter where you are headed within the country, you are bound to run into some kind of paranormal event...

When it comes to cemeteries, we all know they are creepy in and of themselves. When it comes to cemeteries that are haunted, we know that the creepiness gets even worse. Now, if you were to combine England with a haunted cemetery, things get as creepy as you can imagine.

The Highgate Cemetery is one of the most haunted cemeteries in the world. It was first established in the early 1800s, and it was considered a very fashionable place to be buried by the Victorian people. This cemetery is incredible to visit, even if you don't have any friends or relatives who are buried there.

With grave stones still in place bearing dates spanning back a couple hundred years, as you walk through this cemetery, you are taken on a trip through time. Each of the gravestones marks the date it was planted, and you can see as you walk through row after row, each gravestone bears the marks of the time it was created.

Even if you don't see a ghost or a paranormal spirit in this cemetery, you can feel the energy is high, and the sadness that hangs in the air is so strong, it's almost as though you can touch it...

By the turn of the 20th century, it was estimated that tens of thousands of people have been buried in that single cemetery, spanning the course of the past 200 years. But, around the turn of the century the cemetery began to fall into neglect, and with no one around to take care of it, the tree roots and shrubs began to take over.

The once impressive monumental headstones now stand at an angle, and the graves that would take your breath away are now cracked with a worn out look to them. It is also interesting to note that the paranormal events that started happening in the cemetery coincide with the decay of the land.

Though there is a lot of speculation surrounding the cemetery, there are many confirmed reports from hundreds of people and the sights that they have seen there. From sightings of single apparitions to entire groups of people at a time, it appears as though this cemetery is alive with a lot more than we realized.

Some of the most common apparitions which appear are varied as well. There is an old man who appears at the northern hill in the cemetery often. He has a long grey beard and a top hat, and he is always walking up the hill. He appears out of nowhere, then he vanishes just as quickly, without any sign of him anywhere…

Then, there's the sighting of the young woman with long, wavy hair. She appears near a specific set of gravestones often, sitting and wrapping her arms around herself. She doesn't ever say anything to those around her, and she doesn't even appear to notice when there are others in the same place.

She sits on the edge of a gravestone, holding herself in her arms and rocking back and forth. As with the old man, she seems to appear out of nowhere and vanish just as quickly, with no form of regularity.

There have been reports of a variety of children throughout the entire cemetery. There are reports of young children who run around the gravestones, and there are other reports of children hiding around the graves and peering out at the guests who are in the graveyard.

In more recent years, there are sightings of a phantom cyclist who rides through the cemetery and disappears into the wall, but in even more recent times there has been a report of a mad old woman appearing throughout the graves.

This woman has only appeared in more recent years, but she doesn't appear to be friendly at all. She is dressed in older clothing with long grey hair, and she wanders through the gravestones. Her dress is ripped and her hair needs to be combed, and it appears as though she is always searching for someone, though no one knows who she is or what she is looking for.

But, if she spies anyone in the cemetery, she covers her ears with her hands and falls to her knees, then she closes her eyes and begins screaming. She screams a high pitched, blood curdling scream that pierces throughout the entire cemetery.

People have heard it from across the cemetery, though they have said that it is difficult to pinpoint where it is coming from. Then there are those who have seen her screaming with their own eyes…

Regardless of where she is when you see her, she always vanishes right after her scream. Paranormal investigators who have specifically waited to find her have tried to scan the area after she disappears, but she is simply gone, vanished into thin air.

There's no way to tell when she's going to arrive, and there are many times when visitors don't realize she's there until she starts her terrible wailing.

It is unknown why new apparitions appear, and why old ones continue to appear even after years of being in the same cemetery. There are times it would appear that these spirits are confined to a certain place in the cemetery, then it would seem that they are only there out of preference.

There is little doubt that these paranormal spirits will continue to wander through this cemetery as the years pass, giving us a glimpse into the unknown with each new sighting.

While no one is certain as to why they do what they do, it is certain beyond a shadow of a doubt that these hauntings are real, easily making London's Highgate Cemetery one of the most haunted cemeteries on the planet...

Chapter 8
The Insane Sanatorium

There's just something inherently creepy about an old hospital, regardless of what it was used for. It seems this creepiness gets worse as time goes by, taking its toll on the building and memories that were made there.

Some of these memories may be happy, but for many, hospital memories are anything but, and the Waverly Hill Sanatorium is no exception to that rule.

This Sanatorium was the site where hundreds of thousands of people passed away, leaving behind families and loved ones in agony. Though many did what they could to help these people, this Sanatorium proves that the paranormal can strike, even when there isn't evil taking place.

The Waverly Hill Sanatorium was established in the year 1910, and though it was used in a variety of ways through the years, the biggest benefit it gave to society was to help ward off the effects of tuberculosis. The terrible disease ravaged the Kentucky countryside, leaving a path of destruction in its wake. This hospital would house thousands of people at a time, and there were recorded instances of entire families residing in the hospital at the same time, and tragically the entire family passing.

Tuberculosis is highly contagious, and wiped out entire towns in its day. It was incredibly important that when there was an outbreak, to contain the illness as much as possible, and try to keep it from spreading.

Which is what those who worked in the Waverly Hill Sanatorium were trying to do.

There is a large tunnel that runs from beneath the hospital back outside. It was necessary to construct it as the death toll reached the thousands, and the nurses couldn't keep up with taking care of the bodies.

They would run the bodies outside through this tunnel, trying to contain the disease and care for those who had died without disrupting the events of the hospital or causing too much distress to those who were still fighting for their lives. Yet in spite of the greatest efforts of these men and women, countless lives were being lost continually as time wore on.

But tuberculosis wasn't the only tragedy that was going on inside the sanatorium, and it isn't just the victims of this tragedy that haunt the place. Perhaps the most famous tragedy the building is known for is what happened in room 502.

A nurse by the name of Mary was found hanging in this room, and the rumor is that her suicide was a result of her discovering she was pregnant outside of wedlock. However, the rumors take a sicker turn as you learn that the father of the child was a doctor in the hospital, who was married...

It is assumed that he tried to perform an abortion on Mary, but ended up murdering her in the process. He then made it appear as though she committed suicide to cover his tracks and keep himself out of trouble.

Another nurse died from exposure to this same room just a few years later as she flung herself out the window and to her death. It is unknown why she did this, but the suspicions which surround this haunted room may have had something to do with it.

One popular rumor which surrounds this event is that she was pushed, but not by any earthly being. She was a kind woman with a very happy life and had no reason to commit suicide, yet she was flung from the window.

Throughout the years, suicides and strange deaths were frequent in the hospital. It seemed that not even a few years could go by without someone doing something to mysteriously take their life, or for someone to be found dead without any real explanation as to how it happened…

But it wasn't until the middle of the 20th century that documented paranormal events began to take place. The room, 502, became a paranormal hot spot, with voices being heard regularly, objects flying off the walls, and shadows being cast when there is no one there to cast them.

The tunnel in which the bodies were shuttled out of is full of voices and some have even reported seeing an apparition from time to time. There are reports of strange sounds coming from the walls when there is no one in the room and scratching taking place behind the doorway.

Though you can visit this sanatorium whenever you like, there is never a time to go when it doesn't feel dark and gloomy inside. Though the lighting keeps the place bright, and there are tons of windows to let in airflow, it feel sad, dark, and dreary in the entire building.

The ghostly apparitions appear at any time of the day or night, though it is far more common to see them in the night rather than during the day. Paranormal investigators have searched the entire building, and have found evidence of activity all over the entire place.

Room 502 continues to be the biggest room for activity, even to this day. Though the tragedies that took place in it happened over a hundred years ago, it appears as though the spirits involved are going to remain in the room for as long as the sanatorium stands...

Chapter 9
The Haunting of the Dolls

One of the biggest things that tends to attract the paranormal are things which cannot be explained. Sure, you might see how it was done, you might see when it was done, and you might see who did it, but when it comes to the paranormal events, you just can't tell what is going on.

One of the most mysterious places on the planet is an incredibly creepy island in the middle of a muddy swamp in Mexico. Though you might not think it sounds too bad, if you were to lay eyes on it, you would quickly realize that this is one of the creepiest places you have ever seen.

And to make matters worse, it's haunted.

I am referring to the Island of the Dolls in Mexico…

Most people agree that there is something creepy about most dolls, and many people agree that they don't like the sight of a lot of dolls in one area. Sure, there are those who argue that dolls are simply dolls, but this doesn't change the fact that many would prefer to not have any, or see a lot in a single area.

The Island of the Dolls is one of the creepiest places on earth, with hundreds of old, worn, and broken dolls lashed to trees and fences, all hanging and watching the world around them.

No one knows where they came from, but they are there, and they are fastened tightly to the trees. Countless teams of paranormal investigators have gone in to the area, and what they found was creepy and unsettling to say the least…

It all started around 60 years ago when a young girl was playing outside. She knew how to swim, and she knew she was also supposed to stay away from the water's edge, but no one quite knows what happened.

This girl was friends with an old man who lived on the island. It wasn't a large island, and this man lived there alone. He was very kind and loved the girl, and viewed her as a grandchild. The girl, in turn, loved him, and the two of them were seen together often.

She ended up in the water, and unable to get herself out again, she drowned. It was a terrible tragedy that shook the community to the core, causing them to wonder what sort of evil was descending on the village...

But, the next day, a resident of the town fished an old doll out of the water. No one in the village had ever seen the doll before, and no one knew where it came from. Believing it to be some sort of sign, he hung it on a tree next to where the little girl had fallen into the water in the first place.

Then the next day, he fished out another doll, and the same thing happened again. No one knew where the doll had come from and no one had ever seen it before. It was just suddenly there, and he was the one who was responsible for it.

Unsure of what to do, he hung it on another tree in the same place.

But the situation continued to happen with more and more dolls coming out of the water, and him hanging them on trees all around the area. No one knew where the dolls were coming from, and everyone was afraid to do anything but hang them on the trees as the old man had done.

Soon, there were old dolls hung all over the island.

Then, one day, the dolls stopped. The old man continued to go to the place where he had been finding them, and day after day he continued to check for more, but the flow of dolls stopped as suddenly as it had begun, and he was left on the island with hundreds of dolls lashed to fences, trees, and anything else he could tie them to...

But then things took a turn for the worse, and the old man was found dead shortly after. It appeared as though something had happened to him, because though he was old, he was in excellent health, but he suddenly passed without warning.

There were rumors that the dolls were possessed by spirits, and that one of the dolls killed him, and there were other rumors stating that another spirit came out of the water, and just as it had killed the little girl, it had killed him as well.

But no one was able to confirm what had happened to the old man, all they could do was sit back and watch what was going to happen to the island.

The Island of the Dolls is a small island, and there aren't a lot of living creatures on it. The old man was the only inhabitant, and with him gone, there was no one there to take care of things... or move anything.

Suddenly, people began to notice strange things happening on the island. Dolls were suddenly in places where they hadn't been before, but they were just as securely latched to the trees as they had been in their previous locations.

Dolls were missing body parts, then they would mysteriously appear once again. Strange sounds would come from the island both in the day and at night, and upon investigation, it was clear that there was no one on the island that could make such noises...

There are reports that the sounds that come from the island aren't like anything any animal could make, as if they sound inhuman, almost like a monster.

Visitors who have braved the island at night report hearing whispers among the dolls, though no one is there to make the voices.

No one knows where these dolls came from, and no one knows why they appeared where they did, but it does appear as though they are a prime place for the paranormal to target, and for as long as they hang on the trees, there will be paranormal activity surrounding the area...

Chapter 10
The Whispers of London's Tower

Some of the creepiest places on earth *are* creepy because of the things that happened in their past, and the Tower of London is no exception to this rule.

The Tower or London is a famous and iconic landmark for London, but not many people actually realize what it was for, and how many people awaited their deaths within its walls...

Of course, we all know that England is one of the most haunted places on the planet, but part of the reason for this is because of an event such as what took place in the London Tower. In this chapter, I am going to show you how even some of the most iconic places on the planet can be riddled with paranormal activity.

The Tower of London was constructed in the year 1078, and it has been a landmark of London's skyline ever since. But, what we see on the outside is nothing compared to what has taken place on the inside...

Henry the eighth was murdered in this tower as he knelt in prayer, bringing his terrible reign to an end. To this day, it is said that on the anniversary of his death, at the precise time he was murdered (about one hour before midnight), you can hear the sound of his voice through the halls of the tower.

The room in which he was murdered holds the most vivid words he utters, and some have been able to hear actual sentences.

There is a haunting "white lady" who can be viewed within various points of the tower. No one knows where she came from or where she was headed, but the distinct smell of her perfume fills the air when she is around, and you can witness her walking the halls of the tower, or waving through the window at something unseen on the other side.

She has been seen on multiple occasions by multiple people, and many are certain that her perfume is a sign that she is about to appear. Various paranormal investigators have walked through the halls, trying to catch a whiff of her perfume simply so they can find her. In spite of this hunting, it doesn't appear as though she can be found, and only shows herself when she feels like doing so.

It is said that the room in which Henry the eighth kept his armor is one where you can feel the physical effects of the paranormal. Guards who have gone into this part of the tower will suddenly feel a crushing feeling on their heads and chests, and they have no idea where it is coming from. The feeling only gets worse until they stumble out of the room, and it is lifted almost immediately.

Another guard reported that as he walked the halls one night, he was passing this room with the armor inside. Suddenly, an unseen assailant grabbed him from behind, and though there was nothing in the room with him, he felt as though there was a cord thrown around his neck and pulled tight…

He fought for his life and managed to get the attacker off, then he ran as quickly as he could to the front of the tower, where he showed his neck to his friend. The marks of the attack were clearly etched into the man's throat, bearing witness that there really had been a paranormal experience in the halls.

The tower also bore countless prisoners as they prepared for their deaths, including the king's wife, Anne Boleyn. She can still be seen in the prison of the tower, walking back and forth on the anniversary of her execution.

Another women whom Henry the eighth had murdered is also still seen in the halls, forever running from her executioner. The story states that King Henry wished to have her son murdered, knowing that the boy was a true threat to the crown. She learned of his plan and had her son removed from the country, so the king had her executed instead.

It is said that when she reached the chopping block, she refused to kneel when she was instructed to, stating she was no traitor, so she wouldn't be executed as a traitor. The executioner wasn't going to let her go, however, and raised his ax to strike her where she stood.

Terrified, the woman turned and ran, but the executioner wasn't going to let her get away. He chased her through the courtyard before hacking her to death in the corner of the yard.

It is said that this apparition can still be seen, both the woman screaming and running, and the executioner chasing her with a raised axe. Many claim to have heard her screams even when she is not present, but, the screams are still penetrating and loud.

The two young boys, Edward the Fourth's sons, were set to take the throne after his death, but Parliament declared they were illegitimate children, and gave the throne to Richard the Third instead.

It is said that these two boys would often go to the tower to play, but the night the older of the two was to take the throne, they went to the tower and never came back. No one knows for sure what happened to them, they simply vanished into thin air.

But now, their spirits can be seen running through the halls of the tower, or their voices can be heard calling to each other through the rooms. Though no one is in the rooms to see them, many have heard their voices...

The grounds around the tower are also filled with their fair share of paranormal activity. Ghostly beings with terrible wounds can be seen from time to time, wandering around the area and looking for someone to help them.

Phantom horses can be heard nearby, and some have even reported seeing a phantom carriage exit the tower and then return again.

As incredible as it is, there are many, many more stories of the hauntings in London's Tower, and this chapter is only able to cover some of the most common. If you ever have the opportunity to visit the tower yourself, keep your eyes open, you never know what you might see...

Chapter 11
The Haunted Secrets of Skirrid Inn

Pubs are one of the most bustling places you will ever witness. People from all over the country, all over the world, can be found in these places, and they each have their own tales and life stories.

Inns and taverns rank among some of the most paranormal places on the planet. And to make it even more interesting, these places don't have to be old and abandoned for the paranormal events to take place. Some of the most famous hauntings are found in some of the most popular pubs across the country, with the top of the list being a small Inn in the United Kingdom.

With all these people passing through these pubs, it's amazing how many occurrences happen within the walls that never get passed out into the public's eye. There are so many people in the area, it's a small wonder that many of the secrets that happen within the walls are kept safely inside.

But in this chapter, we are going to pull some of the Skirrid Inn's secrets to the light.

Perhaps the most haunted place in all of South Wales, this Inn has many paranormal events take place inside it every year. These events have become so common, many people travel to the area merely to go on a ghost hunt.

And many find more than they bargain for.

The Inn was a reputably violent place where fights were almost as common as the drinks that were being served. The entire Inn holds such a dark feeling that many people refuse to spend the night there, though it's still available for you to do so if you choose.

The ghosts who haunt the Skirrid Inn are not at all friendly, and there is a history of them ripping things off the walls and throwing them across the room. Men and women report lying in bed and feeling their sheets getting torn off them from the foot of the bed, and when they look to see who is there, the room has no one in it besides them.

There are reports of photos randomly shaking on the walls when there is no one there to touch them, and there are reports of things being moved about within the Inn and the rooms upstairs, even when there has been no one in the room the entire day.

The sinister atmosphere lends to the creepiness of the Inn, and the odd laughter that rattles the windows and echoes through the halls is enough to give the hearer nightmares for weeks...

A group of paranormal investigators in 2011 got to experience all of this firsthand as they went on their own ghost hunt within the pub. They were duly warned that the place was full of paranormal activity, and that many of the things that went on inside the pub were violent.

They were assured that this was not the ghost hunt for the faint of heart, and that only those with strong nerves would make it through the night. Undeterred, the group decided to press on, setting up their gear in several rooms throughout the upstairs of the pub.

They set up thermometers, cameras, and sensors. They hung bells on doors and set up their own little base camp to wait and watch, ready to see what was going to happen...

This group had been through several paranormal experiences, but they had never seen anything that would convince them that the paranormal could actually be dangerous, until that night at the Inn.

As they sat, things started happening slowly. The air would suddenly get as cold as ice, and they would put on their jackets or button their coats to ward off the sudden change in temperature.

Then, the doors would begin to move slowly. Some would open slightly, some could close, but all moved enough to set off the ringing of the bells. The group was impressed but they weren't certain that these events were paranormal, or if they were a result of the windows being open or drafts running through the house.

But that was just the beginning.

By midnight, items on the walls began to shake and turn. Photos that had been hanging out of the way of any drafts would fall to the ground and shatter. The doors that had opened slowly were now slamming closed or flying open so quickly it was impossible for the bell to stay on.

But to make matters worse, the ghosts didn't want to be filmed, and the crew discovered that each and every one of their cameras had been thrown violently to the ground. It was evident that whatever had knocked them over didn't just knock them down, it threw them to the ground with such force the lenses cracked on each and every one.

The crew were sure they were going to make it through the night, but when the cameras started breaking, they realized that it was dangerous for them to stay, and decided to quickly pack up and leave.

But that was when the footsteps started. It sounded as though someone who was very heavy, was running across the floorboards above them, but when they raised the door to the attic, it was clear that there was nothing up there, not even a box.

They walked back downstairs, but the footsteps continued to run across the floor, sending chills down their spines every time.

The group left the Inn as quickly as they possibly could, each one personally vowing they would never return to that haunted place.

When the bartender was told the events of the previous night the next morning, he confirmed that those were the normal things that happened on an almost nightly basis.

These same reports are given by most who stay in the Inn, and many who leave vow they will never return...

Chapter 12
The Demon of the Close

Though the United Kingdom and England tend to have greater focus placed on them when it comes to paranormal events, anywhere in the world can have this kind of occurrence, and we are going to wrap up our investigation with the demons found in a close in Scotland.

As I have said before, it can be hard to know the difference between a demon and a ghost, and sometimes you can only measure by how violent the apparition is, but with this story, it's pretty evident what we are dealing with.

In Europe, a close is a type of shelter which was originally built for safety and protection during air raids in the war. People would flee to these rooms where they would be safe in an underground location until the raid was over, when they would come back out to see what the damage was to the rest of the city.

These can be seen dotting the towns of Europe from one country to the next, and to this day many of them are still accessible, though they have largely been converted into other things.

But just because these closes were in place for safety, it didn't mean they always did their job, and many times they were the scene of many crimes that took place in the area. They were down, out of the way, and underground, so it was an easy place to drag a victim.

However, many of the closes also had locks on the front of them, so to get inside one, you had to know the lock combination or have a key.

There was a man in Scotland during the time of WWII. He was a key maker, and one who was well sought after for his ability to make good keys, and to make them quickly. He would be one of the first people these owners would turn to to make new keys for their houses and safety zones.

But, Brodie was a depraved and perverse man, and he would make double keys for every close that he secured. He would have access into everyone's homes as well as their safety houses, and would use his duplicate keys to break in and do unthinkable things to the people inside...

There were times he would merely steal from the family, but there were others when he would commit crimes against the women in the household, or beat old men. It is rumored that he even murdered elderly couples and took what he could from their houses under the cover of night.

He was good at covering his tracks, and it was a long time before the authorities were able to catch up with him. Because of the terrible nature of each of his crimes he was sentenced to death immediately, and his execution was placed for the next day.

He was hanged until dead, and his body was buried in a small cemetery outside of Scotland. But he wasn't done with the world yet...

It has been reported that Brodie's apparition still appears in several of the closes that he would frequent, including the Royal Mile close in the downtown area.

His apparition is said to be terrifying. He is reported to be dressed completely in black from head to toe, but dressed in business attire as he did when he was alive. He has a key ring with dozens upon dozens of keys on it, and you can hear them jingle as he walks through the small safety shelters.

But perhaps the most terrifying thing of all is that his neck still bears the marks of the rope from which he was hanged, and it is reported that he rides a black horse with flames coming out of its nostrils and fire in its eyes…

There are times when they see his entire apparition, there are times when they see his shadow on the wall, then there are times when they don't actually see him, but they report that they hear the jingling of his keys as he tries them on the locks to the close.

Though he isn't seen often, when he is spotted, the people of the town all agree that he is one of the most terrifying things they have ever laid their eyes on.

There doesn't appear to be any real pattern to where he appears or when, and no one knows for sure why he frequents the Royal Mile Close as much as he does, but for those who are in Scotland, visiting this small safety shelter is well worth your time.

Keep your eyes open, and you may see Brodie for yourself…

Conclusion

There you have it, some of the most haunted stories from some of the creepiest places on earth. I hope this book opened your eyes to some of the strange events you never realized happened in these famous locations, and that someday you may have the opportunity to experience some of these events for yourself.

No matter where your travels take you, keep an open mind for what could happen, and a watchful eye for seeing the events first hand. You never know when something paranormal could occur, and if you aren't paying attention, you could miss it.

Spirits and ghosts are all around us, whether you notice them or not. I hope this book opens your eyes to how prevalent they really are, and how frequently they interact with people still living in the world.

Keep a watchful eye, and your paranormal experience could be next...

If you enjoyed this book, do you think you could leave me a review on Amazon? Just search for this title and my name on Amazon to find it. Thank you so much, it is very much appreciated!

Take a Look at Some of My Other Books

Below are some of my other popular books that are popular on Amazon. Most are in Print and Audio versions to. You can visit my author page on Amazon to see other work done by me, or just search my name on Amazon (Roger P. Mills) and the book title to find them.

Ouija Board Stories

Ouija Board Stories – Book 2

True Bigfoot Stories

True Horror Stories

Haunted Asylums

Haunted Places

Missing People

Haunted Dolls

True Hauntings and Paranormal

Horror

Horror Stories

Want to get your free books?

Yes that's right, we send free books out to our subscribers every single week!

If you think that sounds pretty awesome, then visit our website below and sign up!

All you have to do then, is keep an eye on your inbox for the next free books for the week.

Enjoy!

        Sign up here: www.LibraryBugs.com

Made in the USA
Lexington, KY
01 February 2018